8/99

O

99

9 x 3/11

D0895667

CHRISTOPHER REEVE

LIBBY HUGHES

TAKING PART

DILLON PRESS
Parsippany, New Jersey

May Christopher Reeve's life be an inspiration to all those who face enormous challenges in life.

Photo Credits
Front cover: AP/Wide World Photos.
Back cover: Sygma Photo News. © 1978 Film Export A.G.

ABC, Inc./Capital Cities/Ken Regan: 13. Camera 5/Ken Regan: 59, 65. CBS: 39. Cornell University Theatre: 33. Superman and all related indicia are trademarks of DC Comics © 1938. All rights reserved: 44. Gamma Liaison Network/Alex Berliner: 67. Michele Houle: 31. Libby Hughes: 28. The Julliard School/Henry Grossman: 37. Joan Lewis, realtor: 22. Terri Miller: 6. Outline/Timothy Greenfield-Sanders: 72. Photofest: table of contents *inset*, 47, 51, 57, 58. Princeton Day School: 24, 25, 26. Rex U.S.A./Dennis Stone: 11. Sygma Photo News: 4; D. James: 53; J. Ohlinger: 48. Williamstown Theatre: 55.

Library of Congress Cataloging-in-Publication Data
Hughes, Libby.
Christopher Reeve / by Libby Hughes. — 1st ed.
       p. cm. — (Taking part books)
Includes index.
ISBN 0-382-39656-1 (lsb). — ISBN 0-382-39715-0 (scr)
1. Reeve, Christopher, 1952–   —Juvenile literature. 2. Actors—United States—Biography—Juvenile literature. [1. Reeve, Christopher, 1952–   . 2. Actors.] I. Title.
PN2287.R292H84 1998
791.43'028'092—dc20
[B]   96-28221
Summary: A biography of stage and screen star Christopher Reeve, whose remarkable courage and grace in dealing with a paralyzing injury have shown him to be a true super hero.

Cover and book design by Michelle Farinella

Copyright © 1998 by Libby Hughes

Published by Dillon Press
A Division of Simon & Schuster
299 Jefferson Road, Parsippany, NJ 07054

First Edition
Printed in the United States of America
10 9 8 7 6 5 4 3 2 1

CONTENTS

Christopher Reeve gained fame as the star of four Superman *movies.*

1

A Horseback-Riding Accident

Memorial Day weekend 1995 would change forever the life of actor Christopher Reeve. Star of four *Superman* movies, Reeve had practiced riding his horse several hours a day six days a week in the months preceding. A special competition was being held in Culpeper, Virginia, and he wanted to be ready for it. Reeve trucked his newly purchased horse, Eastern Express, from his home in Bedford, New York, to Culpeper. The drive would take six or seven hours—perhaps longer, pulling a horse trailer.

Virginia is a beautiful state. The hills roll and twist like the waves of the sea. The grass seems greener and the clouds almost touch the crest of each hill. Less than 50 miles from Washington, D.C., Culpeper is known as the heart of horse country. Here the farmlands fan out in every direction. Behind white fences and gray fences, horses swish their tails and graze contentedly in deep green fields. Farmhouses of sturdy fieldstone sit majestically on knolls, overlooking the land and horses.

From March through November, the people of

Christopher Reeve rides Eastern Express on a summer day.

Culpeper watch convoys of horse trailers passing through the camel hump of their main street and heading for Commonwealth Park, six miles from the center of town. Business prospers during these months.

Flanked by the famous Blue Ridge Mountains in the distance, Commonwealth Park stretches over 210 acres. It is the third largest facility of its kind in the United States. Within the sparsely wooded land are seven show rings, tennis courts, restaurants, a saddle shop, and a swimming pool. The 900 stalls in the rows of stables are leased to the owners of visiting show horses. Christopher Reeve unloaded Eastern Express and led him into one of those stalls.

Monk Reynolds, the owner of Commonwealth Park, had leased his grounds to the Commonwealth Dressage and Combined Training Association for their three-day spring trials. Dressage is a specialized and precise form of show competition. The measured prancing steps by the horse in a dressage competition are produced by controlled movements by the rider—a most difficult skill. But Reeve had been competing for eight years and hoped to qualify in the cross-country competition on Saturday afternoon after completing the dressage in the morning.

Saturday, May 27, was pleasant. The sun was shining, and it was hot and humid, as Virginia can be in the spring. Many of the 300 competitive riders were wiping the perspiration from their faces. The smell of newly mown grass filled the air as did the musty aroma of wet horse hair and the crunching sound of leather saddles.

In the morning, Christopher Reeve wandered into the Show Cafe, one of the many cocoa-colored buildings trimmed in dark chocolate brown. He stood in line to order breakfast. He was wearing off-white riding breeches, high boots, and a T-shirt. At 6 feet 4 inches and 200 pounds, he was soon recognized as Christopher Reeve, the movie star. A group of women surrounded him, asking for autographs. He chatted comfortably with them and scrolled his name across the back of one of their T-shirts. They were impressed by his lack of snobbishness.

By midafternoon, Reeve was fully dressed in his blue and silver colors, familiar to the horseshow participants. Despite the heat he wore a safety vest under his formal jacket and shirt. He also wore a safety helmet, another requirement. Gradually he warmed up on his 12-year-old chestnut horse, Eastern Express.

Then his number was called, and Reeve began the 15-hurdle, two-mile cross-country course. According to observers, his rhythm was fine, and he cleared the first two hurdles without any problem. The third jump was a zigzag log fence that was only three feet three inches high. His approach was good. He and Eastern Express were galloping at a good speed. Reeve leaned over the neck of Eastern Express to take the jump. The horse's front legs lifted and his hooves touched the top log, but his back legs never left the ground. Eastern Express stopped and refused to go over the hurdle. The reason is unclear. Whether he was spooked by the weight of his rider or the dashing movement of a rabbit from the underbrush is not known.

But Christopher Reeve sailed over the horse's neck and head. His hands were caught in the reins, causing a flip fall. Reeve hit his forehead on one of the fence logs and then hit the ground with the full force of his 200 pounds on his neck. Reeve's body crashed to the earth and lay very still.

The competition stopped. One of the safety officials at the competition, Helmut Boehme, rushed to Reeve, who was unconscious and not breathing. Among the spectators was an anesthesiologist, who came to help and cleared Reeve's air passages. Rescue squads were called, and Reeve was quickly transported to Culpeper Memorial Hospital. Once Reeve's breathing was stabilized, he was shuttled to a helicopter and flown to the University of Virginia's Medical Center in Charlottesville. Doctors there, specializing in vertebrae and spinal-cord injuries, were more qualified to care for Reeve's injury.

The world was stunned. Their hero, Superman, the Man of Steel, paralyzed? It couldn't be. No one wanted it to be. Prayers and well wishes flooded the hospital. Cards, telegrams, and notes over the Internet were overwhelming.

News reporters from all over the world descended on

the university to monitor the actor's progress. Members of Reeve's family were gathered in the waiting room and at his bedside. Among the first to arrive were his mother, Barbara Johnson; his father, Franklin D. Reeve; and his wife of three years, Dana Morosini Reeve. His former partner, Gae Exton, and their two children, Matthew, 16, and Alexandra, 12, came from London. Family members were cautious about allowing too much detailed information to be released to the public.

The kind of fall Reeve suffered is fairly common to riders during their riding careers. If Reeve had not been tangled in the reins, his hands would have stretched in front of him and broken the fall. Consequently the 42-year-old actor might have brushed off the dirt and remounted. But the entanglement caused the unusual complications.

When Dr. John A. Jane, Reeve's neurosurgeon, finally spoke to the public, he explained the extent of Reeve's injuries. During the accident Reeve had received multiple fractures to his first and second cervical vertebrae, resulting in apparent paralysis from the neck down. In order to breathe he would need a respirator. Once his spine was stabilized, a major operation to remove the shattered bone pieces and fasten the broken vertebrae would be performed.

Gae Exton (center), *with children Matthew and Alexandra, arrives from London shortly after Reeve's accident.*

In the United States there are approximately 250,000 people with similar spinal-cord injuries. As many as 10,000 similar injuries a year can happen from horseback riding, diving, motor vehicle accidents, or sports accidents. If the brain is not damaged, many people who are quadriplegic can lead happy and successful lives.

11

On the Wednesday after the Saturday fall, Christopher Reeve regained consciousness. Without remembering what had happened, his first thought was, "This can't be me!" For a few minutes he thought it might be too much of a burden on other people to take care of him. Then, his wife, Dana, came to his bedside. He asked her if she still wanted him this way.

"You're still you and I love you" was her answer.

In a television interview with Barbara Walters, Dana said, "When it's actually the person you love, the person you know and there's no head injury, no brain damage, it's him, it's the essence of him, and that's what I said to him . . . I also said, though, of course, that it was his decision, but that I would be here for the long run— no matter what, no matter what had happened, I would be there . . . "

Dana told Walters that when the children walked into the room—Matthew, Alexandra, and Will, Dana and Christopher's three-year-old child—his decision was made.

Christopher told Walters, "I could see how much they needed me and wanted me. What happens to me when I have a problem is I get embarrassed. I go like, oh, I don't want to cause you people trouble, and I don't want people to be burdened to take care of me, you know? That was

*Christopher Reeve in a television interview with
Barbara Walters after his accident*

my thought briefly on that afternoon, and the minute they
all came in and I could see the love and feel the love and
know that we're still a family. . . the thought vanished, and
it has never come back again."

Coincidentally, earlier in 1995, Reeve had played the
part in an HBO movie of a police officer who was

paralyzed by a gunshot wound. To research the part for his role in *Above Suspicion*, Reeve had gone to a trauma center for those with spinal-cord injuries. He was amazed at how easy it was to receive such injuries.

On June 5, Dr. Jane performed a six-hour operation to secure Reeve's head to his spine through the insertion of rings and a rod. He removed shattered bone fragments and took shavings from Reeve's hipbone to insert between the vertebrae. The operation was a success, and Christopher Reeve began his recovery.

On June 9, Dana Morosini Reeve made a public statement from the University of Virginia Medical Center.

> *I am here to express Chris's and my sincere thanks to everyone who has been helping us through this very difficult time... Chris's spirits are for the most part quite good... He has already begun the first stages of physical and occupational therapy.*
>
> *Much of his day is spent listening to messages sent from well-wishers. I can't begin to express how important these are to him. Chris is a man blessed with extraordinary inner strength. He is a passionate man, committed to doing things well. I can't think of a challenge he has not met... with fervent gusto. He is a fighter and a survivor*

of the first order. But this has to be the toughest challenge he has ever faced. I know it is mine.
    He is honored by the good wishes sent by President and Mrs. Clinton and many others in public office around the country and the world.

In an interview with Larry King, Chris humorously related how he was talking by telephone to his sister, when Dana kept interrupting to say that the White House was calling on another line and that he should get off the phone. Thinking it was a joke, he continued chatting with his sister. When he had hung up the phone, he discovered that this other call had indeed been the White House. President Clinton had planned with Dana to call at a particular time because he wanted to convey his thoughts and prayers directly to Reeve.

The President wrote Reeve a letter instead. Since then, they have talked about the necessity for more funding for research in the area of spinal-cord injuries. The benefits from Medicare and Medicaid are not enough to pay for the high cost of care. For the special equipment and for 24-hour attendants that are necessary for people with such injuries, the base price each year is $400,000. Reeve's wheelchair alone costs $40,000 and an elevator for his house, $70,000. Reeve is covered by his insurance for two years. After that, he must find a way to pay for his care.

Contrary to common belief and as a result of bad investments in the 1980's, Reeve is not a wealthy man. Rumors circulating that his good friend, actor-comedian Robin Williams, might pick up the tab were false. Supposedly, the two had made a pact while roommates at the Juilliard School in New York that if anything happened to one of them, the other would bear the cost of care. They both have denied such an agreement. Reeve has admitted he owes Williams an emotional debt of friendship, but nothing in the way of money.

Christopher Reeve was soon moved to the Kessler Institute for Rehabilitation in West Orange, New Jersey, for 24 weeks of intensive therapy. What would his future be? Could this man who once played Superman become a super hero of the human spirit and take on another kind of heroic role?

Some answers may come from Christopher Reeve's past. What was he like as a boy, a young man, a seasoned actor? How did he get to be the famous Superman of the movies? What were the influences and qualities of character that shaped him for meeting the challenges resulting from Memorial Day weekend of 1995?

CHAPTER

2

The Tallest Kid

Christopher Reeve's parents seemed picture-book perfect. They both came from prominent families whose fathers were connected to the legal profession.

As a young woman, Barbara Lamb—Chris's mother—was tall, slender, beautiful, strong, and independent. Chris's father, Franklin D. Reeve, had the physique and dark handsome looks of a matinee idol. Both were well-educated: Barbara attended Vassar College, and Franklin was a Princeton University undergraduate, who later earned his MA and PhD at Columbia University. Apparently, Franklin swept Barbara off her feet in a whirl-wind romance. They married and moved to New York City where he taught Slavic languages and creative writing at Columbia University while working on his PhD.

Their first son, Christopher, was born in New York City on September 25, 1952. Their second son, Benjamin, was born a year later. Caring for two active toddlers in the city was a challenge. Christopher Reeve jokingly says that his interest in flying started in

Manhattan when, as a child being pushed in a stroller, he looked up above the tall buildings to the sky beyond, where he saw airplanes. He wanted to be in one and fly it.

Somehow Barbara and Franklin's marriage began to fail, and by the time the boys were three and four, Barbara moved out. She moved with her sons to Princeton, New Jersey, and became a writer and assistant editor for the local weekly newspaper, *Town Topics.* Franklin would continue to teach Slavic languages and creative writing at Columbia before moving to Connecticut to teach at Wesleyan University. He also would become the author of many books, both fiction and nonfiction, as well as poetry.

Barbara and Franklin's divorce was not pleasant. Christopher and Benjamin shuttled between their parents on weekend visits. For 15 years they were caught in the middle of bitter feelings between their mother and father.

However, living in Princeton brought happiness back into Barbara's life. She met Tristam B. Johnson, a Yale University graduate, and they married in June of 1959. Johnson, an investment broker, was a man of immense integrity, active in community affairs. He had four children from another marriage—Kate, Tristam II, Tom, and Beth. Soon the Johnsons would add two more boys to their family, Jeffrey and Kevin, who looked very much like Christopher and Benjamin. Sadly, after 25 years, this marriage also ended.

Meanwhile, Franklin Reeve also remarried. He and his second wife had two boys, Mark and Brock, and a daughter, Allison. While growing up, Christopher Reeve would have stepbrothers and stepsisters and half brothers and a half sister from two families.

For Christopher Reeve, Princeton was an ideal community in which to spend his early years. Life then as now revolved around Princeton University, founded in 1746. The university's black iron gates open onto Nassau Street, the town's main street. Behind the gates are Victorian buildings, impressive Gothic structures, and a wide quadrangle, or open area. The academic atmosphere permeates the town, which has grown to a little over 12,000. Princeton's shops and buildings have a Tudor flavor and cater to the preppy tastes of the students. It was in this affluent and intellectual environment that Christopher Reeve grew up.

In a television biography about her son, Barbara Johnson recalled that at five years old he was desperate to play ice hockey on the Pee Wee hockey team. Every Saturday morning he was up early and at the rink, dressed and practicing. He begged the coach to let him play, and finally the coach gave in and let him play goalie. Christopher's determination and true grit began early.

Tristam Johnson fondly remembers Christopher and Benjamin playing well together in both their Hawthorne Avenue and Westcott Road homes. "Both boys were always large in size and shape. They were imaginative. One time they were in the basement, putting together a model train. Ben was the electrician and laid the track. He could fix anything. They had a map on the wall, showing where the train was going," said Mr. Johnson.

Despite the outward appearance of happiness, Chris suffered inwardly from his mother and father's divorce. He felt used as a pawn by both of them. To escape the parental battle, he threw himself into many sports and activities where he could forget the pain of their relationship. Swimming, sailing, skiing, piano, and acting were some of these.

Throughout his elementary and middle-school years, Chris attended the all-male Princeton Country Day School, founded as a private school for the sons of professors at Princeton University. Students here wore coats and ties to classes. Wesley McCaughan taught Chris reading and comprehension courses in the fifth and sixth grades. "I remember him as a delightful young boy, a good student, cooperative, and respected by the boys," said Mr. McCaughan. "In high school, if you passed him in the corridors, he always greeted you with a big grin. He was an all-American boy."

Two miles from the center of town, another exclusive private school was established in 1965—Princeton Day School. The all-boys Princeton Country Day School had merged with the fashionable Miss Fine's School for girls. A thousand acres were given to the school as a gift and provided classroom buildings and many sports facilities for the 570 students. Chris attended this new school from 1965 to 1970.

A perfectionist from an early age, Chris was very often first in his class academically. When he was eight or nine, someone from the famous McCarter Theatre in Princeton came to the school looking for a volunteer to sing a small role in Gilbert and Sullivan's operetta *Yeomen of the Guard*. From his science class Christopher quickly raised his hand and was given the part. Thus began his long journey into the theater.

There were happy times during the summers. Only 50 miles from Princeton was the New Jersey shore town of Bay Head, where Mr. Johnson's brother had a large

*Chris spent many happy times at the Johnson family
summer home in Bay Head, New Jersey.*

rambling house on exclusive East Avenue. Surrounded
by sand dunes and facing the Atlantic Ocean, the house
could easily sleep 27 people. All members of the Johnson
family could use it. They belonged to the yacht club,
where Christopher and his family sailed in races on
Barnegat Bay, which led to the Atlantic Ocean. Later in
life Christopher would own a 46-foot sloop that he
sailed from Nova Scotia to Martha's Vineyard, off the
coast of Massachusetts.

The Bay Head beaches were beige, beautiful, and clean. There were no bars or restaurants in the town. With so many cousins to play with, Christopher and his relatives never lacked for entertainment. The big house was an anchor for everyone; the families were drawn back every summer.

Christopher's eighth-grade English class was taught by Anne Shepherd. Together the class wrote an original play called *Love Conquers All*. "There were two episodes," Mrs. Shepherd recalled. "One was from the Greek era, and the other was from the American West. Chris had the lead role in both. He wore a white toga for the Greek one. He was always more mature than the others. As a leader, he was captain of the hockey team and head of the drama club in high school. During those years he had roles in *Our Town, The Skin of our Teeth, Little Mary Sunshine, Picnic, Watch on the Rhine* . . . He could sing. He had a wonderful voice."

By the time he was 14, Christopher had topped the measuring chart at 6 feet 2 inches. As a somewhat shy and overly tall teenager, he preferred acting in shows on weekends to risking rejection by girls when asking them out. On the other hand, he discovered that acting in plays was sometimes a good way to get a date if a girl came to see him in a play.

Christopher (second from left) *had the lead role in his eighth-grade play.*

By now the love of theater was in his blood. During the summer between ninth and tenth grades, he took a course at the Lawrenceville School in the next town. Christopher's stepfather had gone to high-school there. Young Chris learned about makeup and stagecraft during the course.

A teacher of dramatics at Princeton Day School soon

Christopher in a high school drama club production

became Christopher's mentor. His name was Herbert McAneny. A graduate of Williams College and Oxford University, "Sir McAneny" (as he was nicknamed) started the school journal, directed plays, and coached soccer and baseball. Known as a gentle and sensitive man, he had been teaching since 1931. McAneny saw and encouraged

25

*Reeve poses with two of his former teachers,
Herbert McAneny* (left) *and Wesley McCaughan,
at a Princeton Day School reunion.*

Chris's emerging talent and directed him in a number of
plays in the school's 400-seat terraced theater.

Pursuing his interest in the theater, at the age of 15,
Christopher Reeve traveled to the northwestern corner
of Massachusetts to become an apprentice at the famed
Williamstown Theatre Festival. Nestled in the Berkshire
Hills, Williamstown is a small New England town of
8,000. It is also the home of Williams College, which
plays host to 4,000 students during nine months of the

year. The town hugs the main highway that comes to a halt at the top of the village green. Here the Williamstown Inn welcomes parents and other visitors with its roaring fires and low-hanging brass chandeliers.

Christopher found Williamstown similar to Princeton, but a little smaller. He felt at home, working at the brick and white-columned Adams Memorial Theatre. As an apprentice he took classes, worked in the box office, built sets, and helped move props. Finally he had a small part consisting of two lines as a businessman in *How to Succeed in Business Without Really Trying*.

Peter Hunt, who became a successful theater and television director, was a lighting designer at the Williamstown Theatre Festival when Chris was an apprentice. "I remember Chris as extremely nice and good-looking. Sigourney Weaver, now a famous actress, was an apprentice, too. I had a good feeling about both of them. When you see kids coming through, you can tell which ones will succeed and their careers take off," recalled Mr. Hunt. "We became close friends through the years when Chris returned to the Williamstown Theatre Festival, and I became artistic director there. We also took up flying about the same time and shared many flying stories together."

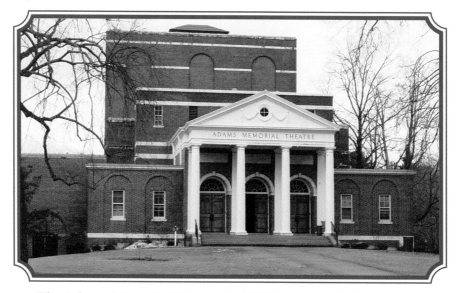

*The Adams Memorial Theatre in Williamstown, Massachusetts,
where the Williamstown Theatre Festival is held*

Once Chris turned 16 he became a member of the
Actors' Equity Association and soon hired an agent. Many
actors have to wait years until they land the professional
part needed to become a member. The next summer
Chris acted at the Loeb Drama Center in Cambridge,
Massachusetts. From there he would go on to do sum-
mer theater at places such as the Boothbay Playhouse in
Maine and California's San Diego Shakespeare Festival.

Christopher Reeve was well on his way to becoming
a professional actor, and in this, his parents encouraged
him. But something else was also important to him—a
college education. Before becoming a full-time actor, he
wanted a complete liberal arts education.

CHAPTER
3

Combining College
and Career

Most high-school seniors wait anxiously for colleges to reply to their applications for admission. Christopher Reeve was one of them. With the help of his eighth-grade English teacher, Anne Shepherd, he had made a number of applications during his junior year. Yale University and Cornell University were among his submissions.

Meanwhile he kept active at Princeton Day School, playing ice hockey, singing with the madrigal group, and performing as assistant conductor of the school orchestra.

Then the letters of acceptance or rejection started arriving: Yale University turned him down, but Cornell University accepted him. He was thrilled. His grandfather had gone to Cornell, and Christopher would continue the tradition.

Chris's theatrical agent was pleased, too, because Ithaca, New York, was not too far from New York City and the theater. This meant that Chris could still go to auditions between classes. In fact, the summer after high-school graduation, his agent found him a role in a national touring company of the play *The Irregular Verb to Love*, starring veteran actor Celeste Holm. Somehow he managed to straddle two worlds—the theatrical and the academic.

Cornell University rises dramatically from the skirts of Ithaca to a rocky perch above the city. Founded by businessman Ezra Cornell in 1865, parts of the university campus remind one of a medieval landscape. Gothic buildings are planted around and across a deep, jagged gorge, with waters gushing below. The bridge across the gorge leads to Risley Hall, a fortresslike structure of dark red stone, that was Reeve's dormitory. Every morning he walked across the bridge to his classes.

The city of Ithaca has its own charm, especially for the university students. On weekends and in their spare time, they walk down the steep streets to the many restaurants catering to the healthy appetites of young students. On the shoreline beyond, stretches picturesque Cayuga Lake, where students and residents sail. A network of paths weaves around the willow trees surrounding the lake. Many young couples stroll hand in hand on the banks of the lake. Nearby, water from a terraced gorge pounds into the deep chasm at its foot.

Above the scenic Cayuga waters, Chris Reeve began

Risley Hall, Reeve's dormitory at Cornell University

his freshman year. He selected English and music theory as his majors. Theater and acting would be a major part of his outside activities.

A pretty Cornell English and theater major, Jennifer Shea, became one of his first steady girlfriends. Shea and Reeve shared an intense love of the theater. To this day the two remain friends.

"Chris had a drive and a dream. He had the drive to

achieve his goals for a career in the professional theater. It was clear what he wanted, and he was not afraid of hard work," she told this author. "He had many talents besides acting. He was a talented musician—playing the piano in the practice rooms in Lincoln Hall. He sang with the chorus and played intramural sports. He is a working actor, not just a star. He believes in the power of art. With all his intelligence, he has a quick wit."

One of Reeve's favorite English professors was Daniel R. Schwarz, who taught an Introduction to Fiction course. Schwarz was direct and honest with his handsome young student. "Chris was articulate, strong, and imaginative—a good student with a B+ average," Schwarz recalled. "He was sincere and decent; his ego was in balance. When he entered class, the women always waited to see where he would sit, and then they would find chairs near him.

"I knew his strengths and weaknesses," continued Schwarz. " I didn't flatter him, but I worked to improve his writing. There was mutual respect between us. He cared about his work, and he was a good actor—not a great actor." After Christopher's accident in 1995, Schwarz was inspired to write a poem about Reeve entitled "Performance."

Christopher Reeve in a performance of Life Is a Dream
while an undergraduate at Cornell

When Professor Schwarz reflected on Christopher
Reeve, past and present, he felt "the man meshed with
the actor." During a visit to Cornell in November 1993,
Reeve gave a keynote address, stressing the need for
promoting and sustaining the arts. Schwarz sat at the
head table next to his one-time student. "He is a resilient
spirit," said Schwarz, "and committed to excellence. He

will make his fiction to live and to become somebody."

While at Cornell, Christopher sometimes found his way to the small theater in Willard Straight Hall. Inside the gray gothic building, the stairs wound down to the basement. There the cement walls on either side of the red chairs for the audience were decorated in murals and frescoes. They showed scenes from Shakespearean plays and had been painted in the 1920s. To one side of the stage was an old black upright piano. According to Marvin Carlson, a member of the theater faculty, Christopher would often come to the theater when it was empty just to play classical pieces on that piano or he would practice in Lincoln Hall.

Professor Carlson remembered Christopher's talent as an undergraduate: "He had the leading role in Calderon's *Life Is a Dream*. This is a poetic play by a Spanish play-wright. We performed it in Lincoln Hall's Black Box Theatre for experimental plays. Chris played the dashing barbaric young man. Compared to the graduate students in the MFA [Master of Fine Arts] program, Chris was very competitive. He had commitment and dedication to his craft. Between rehearsals he would try out new ideas and bring them back to the next rehearsal. Obviously he was a serious actor and a fine team worker."

During his visit to Cornell in 1993, Christopher Reeve talked to both students and faculty about acting and a career in the theater. He encouraged theater students to develop a "love of language." He said, "Acting is the journey of discovery. It's the journey of unlocking the imagination, of finding out about the aspects of living that you didn't previously understand." He also urged the students to be "inquisitive about other cultures."

While a student at Cornell, Reeve wanted to expand his knowledge and be exposed to European culture and theater. Cornell allowed him to spend a semester abroad so that he could become a backstage observer at the Old Vic Theatre in London and the Comédie Française in Paris. He wrote a paper about the experiences and gained credit from Cornell. Furthermore, the university permitted him to apply to the Juilliard School of Drama in New York City in their advanced program. Thus, he spent his entire senior year at Juilliard and was given full credit from Cornell and received his Bachelor of Arts degree from Cornell.

Juilliard would prove to be the springboard to an unbelievable future.

4

From Soap Opera to Superman to Stardom

Every night the glamour and glitter of New York City's West Side come to life at Lincoln Center for the Performing Arts. The square plaza is aglow from the lights shining through the tall arches outside the Metropolitan Opera House and through giant sheets of glass in front of the New York State Theater and Avery Fisher Hall.

Also part of the center is Alice Tully Hall and the Juilliard School, a modern five-story building, layered like a rectangular cake in concrete slabs. The school houses classrooms and performing spaces for students of music, dance, and drama. Once inside, the sounds of musical instruments and actors' dialogue travel up and down the corridors.

Here Christopher Reeve would perfect his talent, working with some of the best acting coaches and directors in the country. Founded in 1905, Juilliard was at first strictly a music conservatory. Only in the late 1960s was a drama division added to the school. Kevin Kline,

The Juilliard School is part of the Lincoln Center for the Performing Arts.

Robin Williams, William Hurt, and Elizabeth McGovern are a few of Juilliard's famous graduates, in addition to Christopher Reeve.

Reeve was fortunate to have been taught by John Houseman, who despite a long and distinguished career in the theater may be best-known to most people from the television series *The Paper Chase*. In the series, Houseman's character was a cantankerous law professor with a hidden heart of gold. Houseman also formed The Acting Company with many Juilliard students.

During his senior year at Juilliard, Christopher Reeve met Robin Williams, the outlandish comedian who later appeared in the movies *Mrs. Doubtfire* and *The Birdcage*. They became lifelong friends. They even shared an apartment with another good friend and actor, Stanley Wilson. Wilson described the three of them this way in an A&E television network biography: "Chris was a preppy, I was a hippy from Texas, and Robin was from Mars!"

To earn some extra spending money, Christopher tried out for the small part of Ben Harper in the soap opera *Love of Life*. He could easily fit this work into his Juilliard schedule. Later, when he became a graduate student at Juilliard, he needed more money for tuition, so he accepted a prominent role in the soap opera. Although Juilliard did

*Christopher Reeve as Ben Harper in an episode
of the soap opera* Love of Life

not encourage such commitments for its students, Reeve did complete his advanced program studies at Juilliard.

The character of Ben Harper was that of a man who loved women, including married women. Often, television viewers fail to make the distinction between actors and the roles they are playing. One time when Christopher was in a restaurant, a woman came over to his table and hit him with her purse for his character's dreadful behavior in the soap opera. Christopher's brother, Benjamin, (who looks very much like Christopher) received similar treatment from a woman who pounded "Ben Harper" on his back with an umbrella for the same reason.

Around this time one of Reeve's drama professors at Cornell, Steve Cole, took a year off from his job to become an off-off-Broadway actor so that he could tell his students what it was like to search for jobs in the professional theater. "From the time he was a student, Chris was the most decent, interesting, and sweet guy," explained Professor Cole. "He was generous and not conceited. He was well-loved by his fellow students and colleagues. And he has become a major citizen of the country and the world."

Once, when Cole met Christopher in the city, they discussed an offer Christopher had received for one of the leading roles in *Cat on a Hot Tin Roof* at the Guthrie Theatre in Minneapolis, Minnesota. At the same time, Christopher was offered a two-line role in a new off-off-Broadway play. The part was that of a Nazi SS officer. He decided to take the small, obscure role. Apparently, he made the right decision. One night the casting agent for *Superman* was in the audience and saw him as a possible player for the movie that would launch him to stardom.

Between events in the soap-opera schedule, Christopher continued to act on the stage at the Circle Repertory Theater and Manhattan Club. By the end of 1975, Reeve landed a small role in the Broadway show *A Matter of Gravity*, starring one of America's most famous actors—Katharine Hepburn. Reeve played her grandson. The show opened in February 1976 but closed in April. A group of his teachers and friends from Princeton Day School went to one of the performances and applauded loudly every time Christopher appeared on stage. An annoyed member of the audience turned around and said, "Why are you doing that? This is a terrible play." According to the drama critics, it *was* terrible. Even the Princeton group agreed with that judgment, but they wanted Christopher to know that they loved him and supported him.

To be in a Broadway play and associated with Katharine Hepburn gave Chris some marketability. He went to California for a minor role in a film called *Gray Lady Down*. But nothing developed immediately for him after that, so he returned to New York City.

Then one day his agent told him about the producers Alexander and Ilya Salkind, who were interviewing actors for the part of Superman. These producers had bought the rights to the *Superman* film in 1974. Since then they had been searching for a star but hadn't found one. Instead, they had recruited famous actors such as Marlon Brando and Gene Hackman for the lesser roles. By 1975 the Salkinds wondered if they should look for an "unknown." Thus, they began their search, auditioning some 200 actors. Until then such stars as Warren Beatty and Burt Reynolds had been considered for the part.

Although not particularly interested in a project based on a comic-book character, Christopher met with the producers as a matter of courtesy to discuss the film. After reading the script, he changed his mind. When he declared his interest, the Salkinds invited him to come to London for a screen test. Reeve's friends thought that if he accepted such a role, his serious acting career would be over. In truth, most of them were jealous.

Before leaving for England, Reeve was the understudy for a leading part in an off-Broadway show. Suddenly the leading man lost his voice, and Christopher had to take over. After that one performance, Christopher had received a standing ovation.

Once the show was finished, he flew to London for the Superman screen test. A thorough actor, Christopher prepared his clothes and makeup for the two different characters—Clark Kent and Superman. For Clark Kent, the clumsy and shy reporter, he wore glasses and an old jacket. His hair was combed differently, and his speech was hesitant. For Superman, he was confident, humorous, and heroic. The stage crew from the screen test gave him the thumbs-up and whispered that he was sure to get the part. Within three days Reeve was on his way back to New York. Soon he heard from his agent. The part was his. He signed a 52-week contract for $250,000, with an additional $5,000 for each week of filming after a year. In fact, the filming took 18 months. Reeve's salary, since he was unknown, was fairly small compared to Marlon Brando's salary of $1 million. Brando had only a brief appearance— as Superman's real father from the planet Krypton.

After Christopher won the part and signed a contract, he telephoned his father, Franklin Reeve, and told him that he was going to play the part of Superman. His father, an academic, mistakenly thought that Christopher meant the role in the play *Man and Superman* by George Bernard Shaw, a famous British playwright. His father was very pleased. When Christopher explained that it was the comic-book character, his father replied with an embarrassed silence.

The Superman comic book originated in 1938 when a man named Jerome Siegel from Cleveland, Ohio, took

Superman is a trademark of DC Comics ©1938

The first Superman comic appeared in June 1938.

his teenage dream and turned it into a smash-hit series. Siegel was basically a shy young man. As a boy, he had wished for the powers of a superman that would make him strong enough to push over buildings and win girlfriends for him. Siegel transformed his idea into a science-fiction story. Once it was finished, he rushed over to the home of his best friend, Joe Shuster, to have him illustrate it. The inspiration for Lois Lane, the reporter who falls in love with Superman, was Lois Amster, the class beauty from Siegel's high school. By 1938 the Superman story became a comic strip. Later, in the 1950s, *Superman* became a popular television series. In the 1990s, after Reeve's *Superman* movies, interest in the character again revived, and a new weekly TV show was created. Today Superman memorabilia is in the Smithsonian Museum.

As Christopher was leaving Princeton for London in a private plane to work on the film, his mother waved goodbye to him from the runway. She felt tears slip down her cheeks. Somehow she knew that her son's life was about to change. Fame and fortune would await him. She was right.

However, when Reeve put on the Superman suit for rehearsals, the producers were not pleased. He was too tall and thin. For ten weeks he ate four meals a day, lifted weights three hours a day, and reshaped his body from 188 pounds to 218 pounds. He made himself into the Superman they wanted.

Before *Superman* hit the movie theaters in 1978, Barbara and Tristam Johnson flew to England to watch some of the filming at the Pinewood Studios outside London. "A 30-second spot, where Superman was under the earth pushing rocks, took almost a whole day," his stepfather recalled. "It was repeated over and over with 50 people helping with lights, powder blower, and complicated techniques."

Because of his youth, athleticism, and strength, Reeve wanted to perform his own stunts. *Superman* was set in a large city called Metropolis, and some of the filming was done in New York City. He and Margot Kidder, who played the reporter Lois Lane, hung in a harness 240 feet above the East River to shoot their flying scenes. Years later, Reeve admitted that he was foolish to have performed some of those dangerous stunts.

Reeve and Margot Kidder fly over Metropolis.

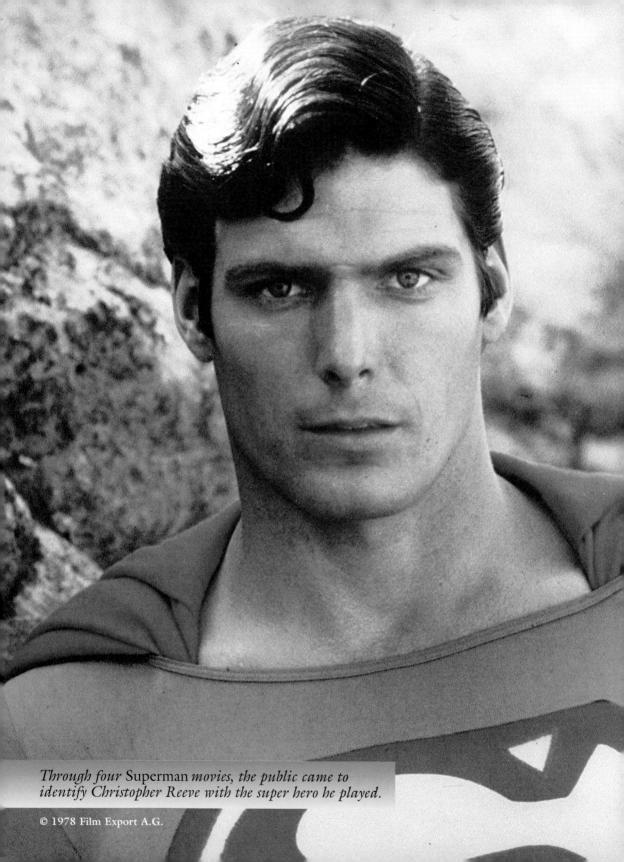

*Through four Superman movies, the public came to
identify Christopher Reeve with the super hero he played.*

CHAPTER

5

Fame, Fatherhood, and the Future

Christopher Reeve rocketed to stardom when the first of four movies about the fictional character Superman premiered in Washington, D.C., in 1978.

The handsome young man with the square-cut jaw and muscular frame could no longer walk down the street unrecognized. To the public he *was* Superman, the hero in blue tights and red cape with a big *S* emblazoned on his chest.

In the plot of the first movie, Superman as a baby is sent to Earth by his parents from the planet Krypton. He lands in the middle of a field in Kansas and is found by a childless couple, who raise him on their farm. After the adoptive father dies, Clark Kent (as Superman has been known) goes to the city of Metropolis to become a newspaper reporter. There he is an awkward young man who secretly changes into Superman whenever there is a need to save someone or fight for truth and justice. The film's musical theme was composed by John Williams, who became a famous conductor and composer. This signature music identified Superman whenever he appeared on the screen.

During the filming of the first movie, Reeve met a young, attractive, English woman who worked for an advertising agency. Her name was Gae Exton. They quickly became a steady couple, and by 1979 their son, Matthew, was born. Reeve enjoyed fatherhood. In 1983 their daughter, Alexandra, was born. Christopher and Gae lived in London for a number of years and had homes in both Los Angeles and New York City. In 1987 they parted, but they remained friends. Often Reeve would spend four months at a time in England to be with his children.

Meanwhile, there was a demand for a sequel to *Superman*. This time Reeve signed a contract for $500,000. *Superman II* was released in the United States in 1981. The story line patterned what was happening in the world—terrorists taking people as hostages. As the movie opens, terrorists have taken 20 hostages in the Eiffel Tower, in Paris, France. Lois Lane has gone to cover the story and climbs up the steel structure to where the hostages are being held. She gets trapped under the elevator, and Superman comes to the rescue. He and Lois plan to marry. Before the marriage he becomes a mortal

A quick change from mild-mannered reporter to super hero

and loses his power. But then, to destroy the evil forces trying to take over the United States, Superman returns to the planet Krypton to regain his powers.

The public wanted still more *Superman* movies. In 1983 the third offering came. This one had more humor. In it, comedian Richard Pryor plays a computer genius, who joins actor Robert Vaughn to take over the world by using computers. Pryor creates a green chemical to destroy Superman. This chemical produces a Superman twin, who is evil. Finally the real Superman is restored.

With the final sequel, *Superman IV* in 1987, Christopher Reeve received more money and had more input into the content of the screenplay than he had in any of the three previous *Superman* movies. In fact, he used the film to project his personal and political views. *Superman IV* was about a quest for peace. In it, Superman speaks to the United Nations about the folly of war; about the threat of nuclear destruction; and about the need to get rid of all nuclear weapons, submarines, and missiles. These are beliefs that Christopher Reeve himself holds.

Of course, there is also plenty of action in the final movie between Gene Hackman and Superman. Hackman's character steals a strand of Superman's hair from a museum and creates a villain with superhuman

In Superman IV *Reeve appeared with Gene Hackman.*

powers. Eventually Superman throws the villain onto
the moon before sending Hackman back to prison.

With each *Superman* sequel, Christopher Reeve
became more famous. During the early days of his
celebrity, Reeve was embarrassed to take limousines to
and from the airport or to special events. He would ask

the limo driver to wait around the corner from his apartment. Finally his friends found out and told him to enjoy his fame. He did. But his ego did not inflate. He remained down to earth and natural.

To keep himself grounded in live theater, Christopher Reeve returned to the Williamstown Theatre Festival in the summers between 1980 and 1994 to perform in 13 classical productions such as *The Cherry Orchard, The Greeks, The Guardsman,* and *Love Letters.* He accepted the same low basic weekly pay ($225) as any other actor for the privilege of performing in familiar surroundings.

His esteem for the theater is reflected in this quote: "If you are serious about professional theater, all roads lead to Williamstown. Somewhere in your past or future, there is the Williamstown Theatre Festival." Eventually Reeve would buy a 40-acre farm in the remote hills above Williamstown.

Between the four *Superman* movies, Reeve received offers to star in a variety of movies, with parts ranging from leading men to villains. Some of the movies he turned down became box-office favorites. They include *American Gigolo* and *Mutiny on the Bounty.* Nevertheless, Reeve's confidence in his acting ability—even after the Superman success—was still not secure. Incredible as it

Christopher Reeve appeared in The Guardsman *at the Williamstown Theatre Festival in 1992.*

may seem, the young star could become tongue-tied and shy in front of talent that he admired.

By 1995, Reeve had appeared in more than 50 films, including television movies and documentaries. In 1980 he starred with Jane Seymour in a film called *Somewhere in Time*. Although this movie was not received well by the critics, many viewers—particularly women—found it enchanting. The story is about a young playwright who wills himself back in time to rekindle a lost love.

From there, Christopher Reeve became a charming villain in 1982's *Deathtrap*. This time he portrayed an aspiring playwright who steals the work of a famous playwright. The same year saw him in a quite different role—Reeve played an ambitious priest in *Monsignor*. In this film, he uses his investment skills for the Vatican, but loses the money to a friend.

Movies based on classical themes appealed most to Reeve. *The Bostonians,* based on the novel by Henry James, was produced in 1984 by British filmmakers Ismail Merchant and James Ivory. The cast included Vanessa Redgrave and Jessica Tandy. The movie was set in Boston in 1875. Reeve played the part of a Mississippi lawyer who falls in love with a feminist.

In 1985, Reeve played the handsome Count Vronsky

Reeve starred with Jane Seymour in Somewhere in Time.

in a movie based on the Tolstoy classic *Anna Karenina*.
Jacqueline Bisset and Paul Scofield were in the cast. Again,
the critics were not very kind to Reeve. Then in 1993,
Reeve played a supporting character to Emma Thompson
and Anthony Hopkins in *Remains of the Day*, another
Merchant and Ivory production. Reeve's character is a
rich American who buys the estate of a Britisher, who
secretly worked with the Germans during World War II.

Whenever an accent was required for a role, Reeve
could reproduce it believably. Whether a southern accent,

Reeve won praise for his role in Remains of the Day.

a British accent, or a Russian accent, his ear for music and flair (like his father's) for languages gave him the ability to master the various distinguishing inflections and pronunciations.

From 1985 to 1995, Christopher Reeve also played in a series of mediocre films such as *The Aviator, Switching Channels, Morning Glory, Above Suspicion*, and a variety of lesser known movies. In 1980 he had some success in a Broadway play called *The Fifth of July*, in which he played a Vietnam veteran whose wartime injuries caused him to be in a wheelchair. Once again he would appear on Broadway in 1989 in *The Winter's Tale*.

Reeve seemed to have reached a plateau and now devoted much of his time to other activities. One of these pastimes was flying, which he did in America and in England. He even flew over to attend the royal wedding between Diana Spencer and Prince Charles. However, the role he most enjoyed was that of father to his two children,

Reeve owned and enjoyed
flying his own airplane.

Matthew and Alexandra. He has definite ideas about raising children. "Give them roots to grow and freedom to fly and never think you own your child—you don't."

In his early days of fame, Reeve was asked who had the greatest influence on his life. He replied that his stepfather, Tristam Johnson, deserved this credit because he had paid for all his schools and had given him "roots and wings."

Now that fame had brought him more money than he had ever dreamed of having, Reeve was able to buy an airplane, a glider, a yacht, and several homes. But he seemed unaffected by fame and fortune.

After he and Gae separated in 1987, Reeve returned to the United States. He re-established his roots and moved forward with his film and theater career. But something far more fulfilling than his professional work would happen to Christopher Reeve in 1987.

Marriage and Facing Tragedy with Courage

During the summer of 1987, Christopher Reeve made a sentimental journey back to the Williamstown Theatre Festival. There he renewed his love of live theater and acted in a play called *The Rover*.

The charm of Williamstown rested happily upon him, especially after his separation from his children. Following weekend performances at the theater, some of the young actors formed a cabaret group. They would perform and sing in the theater or at various restaurants around town.

On one particular evening, Christopher joined a few friends to watch the cabaret talent. A young woman caught his eye. She had straight brown hair, soft brown eyes, and a smile that lit up her face and the stage. She could sing, too. The name in the program read "Dana Morosini." Christopher wanted to meet her. He did and he was enchanted. But when Dana was introduced to him, she resisted his attentions because she had heard that he was a ladies' man. He kept trying. One evening they met unexpectedly and started talking. They stood for one hour talking, and then Dana accepted Reeve's invitation to go out with him. Within a few months they were a steady item. Though Dana was eight years younger, their common interests bridged the age gap. Christopher had never been happier.

As their relationship grew, Reeve combined movies, documentaries, and theater with speaking out on national and international issues. He became involved in activities that included helping children from broken homes, working for the Special Olympics, campaigning for a cleaner and safer environment, saving the whales, and supporting the National Endowment for the Arts. He even went to South America to defend the freedom of writers in Chile to publish articles critical of that country's dictatorship. By lending his celebrity to the writers' group, he helped to save them from being jailed or put to death.

By 1992, Christopher Reeve was certain that he wanted to marry Dana. Over a candlelit dinner of turkey and meatballs in his penthouse apartment in New York City, each came to the same conclusion about their future together—marriage. They planned the ceremony to be in Williamstown and wrote their own vows. Reeve's son, Matthew, would be best man; his daughter, Alexandra, would be maid of honor. Ever since their marriage and the birth of their son, Will, Reeve has called Dana his "life force."

Reeve continued to speak publicly about his views on social and cultural issues. In March of 1995, he appeared at a congressional breakfast to inform members of Congress about the Creative Coalition, which he helped to establish and of which he is co-president. The purpose of the organization is to link education with the arts. In his speech, Reeve said, ". . . there is a crucial role for the government to play in developing the arts and culture in this country."

Only two months later, in May, Christopher Reeve's life would take a dramatic turn. For many years he had trained competitively to enter horse shows. On that Memorial Day weekend in 1995, a horseback-riding accident turned him into a quadriplegic.

During a dark moment for Reeve, a Russian doctor entered his room at the University of Virginia Medical Center. The doctor fussed and fumed and did an unorthodox examination. Suddenly Christopher Reeve was laughing. His good friend Robin Williams had come in disguise to cheer him up. From then on, Reeve knew he was going to be all right.

In an interview with Barbara Walters during his 24 weeks of physical therapy at the Kessler Institute, Reeve confided to Walters, ". . . You see, the first two months after my injury, the demons would get me in the middle of the night. The hours between 2:00 A.M. and 7:00 A.M. are the worst. In my dreams I'd be whole, riding my horse and playing with my family. And suddenly I wake up and it's two in the morning and I'm lying in bed and I can't move and I'm on a ventilator. You know, man, am I lucky. I am so lucky it is unbelievable. You gradually discover, as I'm discovering, that your body is not you and the mind and the spirit must take over and that's the challenge as you move from obsessing about 'why me?' to 'what is the potential?' "

In other interviews Reeve expressed great delight in his three-year-old son, Will, who would jump on the wheelchair and pretend to use it as a go-cart. Will helped with the exercises that his father went through every day to keep his muscles toned. During a wistful moment, Will told his father he liked the way things were before the accident, and Reeve agreed but said they had to move forward.

To accommodate Christopher's wheelchair, the Reeve house in Bedford, New York, was remodeled, with ramps,

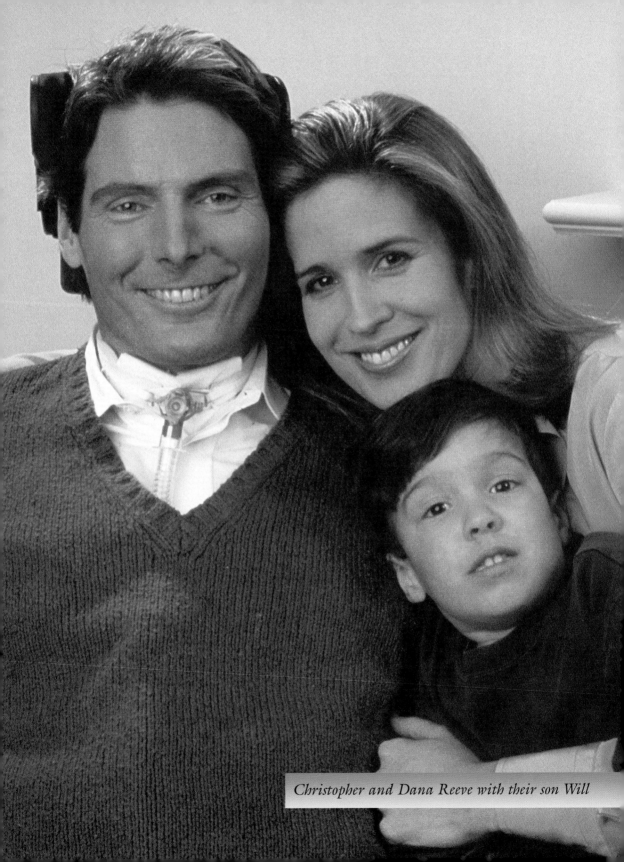

Christopher and Dana Reeve with their son Will

wider doors, and a new wing. A two-car garage was turned into an exercise room. Nurses provided 24-hour care so that the full burden would not fall upon Dana Reeve, allowing her to continue her career in theatrical shows off-Broadway.

Within the first year after his accident, Reeve began actively working for the American Paralysis Association and was appointed to its board. A research center for spinal-cord injuries was named after him at the University of California-Irvine. He made public appearances around the country and gave speeches to raise funds and to pressure the government into increasing funds to Medicaid. Whether insurance companies will raise their lifetime cap of $1.2 million to $10 million is still unknown.

A memorable moment came on Oscar night in March of 1996. In Los Angeles, California, Reeve made an appearance at the Academy Awards, at which members of the Academy of Motion Picture Arts and Sciences honor the best actors, writers, directors, and so on for the preceding year. Reeve's was a surprise appearance. Sitting in his wheelchair at the very back of the stage, Christopher Reeve used his breath machine to move the chair forward. Before he could speak, the whole

Robin Williams poses with Christopher and Dana Reeve at the Governor's Ball following the 1996 Academy Awards.

audience rose to its feet and applauded for nearly five minutes. Tears were in the eyes of many. But mostly they applauded his courage. Reeve is well-loved in the Hollywood community.

Getting to California from New York had taken two

months of planning. Warner Brothers offered its private airplane to transport Reeve, five doctors, and his family to the event. He checked into the hotel under a different name. A special route and a series of ramps were prepared for his secret entry into the theater.

Reeve delivered an important message to his professional colleagues and to the world. He challenged Hollywood to take risks in making films that deal with social issues—issues that stir the social conscience. Afterward, Christopher and Dana met privately with some of their closest friends.

In the future, Christopher Reeve will continue to be a spokesperson for spinal-cord injury research and to serve as president of the American Paralysis Association. On May 15, 1996, Reeve, accompanied by a large entourage of medical personnel, traveled to Washington, D.C., to lobby Senators and members of Congress for increasing funds in this field of research.

In the field of theater and movies, Reeve continues to receive offers. Producers want him to direct a romantic film called *Tell Me True* when he is ready, and he has been offered other directorial assignments as well. Reeve has signed a contract with Warner Brothers to do the voice-over of King Arthur in an animated film, *The Quest for*

Camelot. He also will appear in a CBS-TV movie entitled *Snakes and Ladders.* Judith Light, star of the television series *Who's the Boss,* will have the starring role. In the movie, Light's son becomes paralyzed from a diving accident. Reeve's character befriends the boy and acts as his mentor. Then, too, Reeve has written his autobiography.

Christopher and Dana also hope to have another child. As far as his physical progress, Reeve has told talk-show host Larry King that he wants to "kick the ventilator out the window." Reeve wastes no time in self-pity. His philosophy is summed up in a statement made by actor Ed Harris in the movie *Apollo 13*: "Failure is not an option."

In his everyday life Christopher Reeve is proving that to be true.

INDEX

ABOUT THE AUTHOR

Libby Hughes is the author of numerous books for young readers, including biographies of Colin Powell, Margaret Thatcher, Benazir Bhutto, and Nelson Mandela as well as historical books on West Point and Valley Forge. She edited Ginger Rogers' autobiography and has interviewed hundreds of celebrities for a chain of newspapers on Cape Cod, Massachusetts. Ms. Hughes has lived and worked as a journalist in Africa and Asia. She now resides on Cape Cod and enjoys showing her champion Rhodesian Ridgebacks.